Sacred Lands of the Southwest

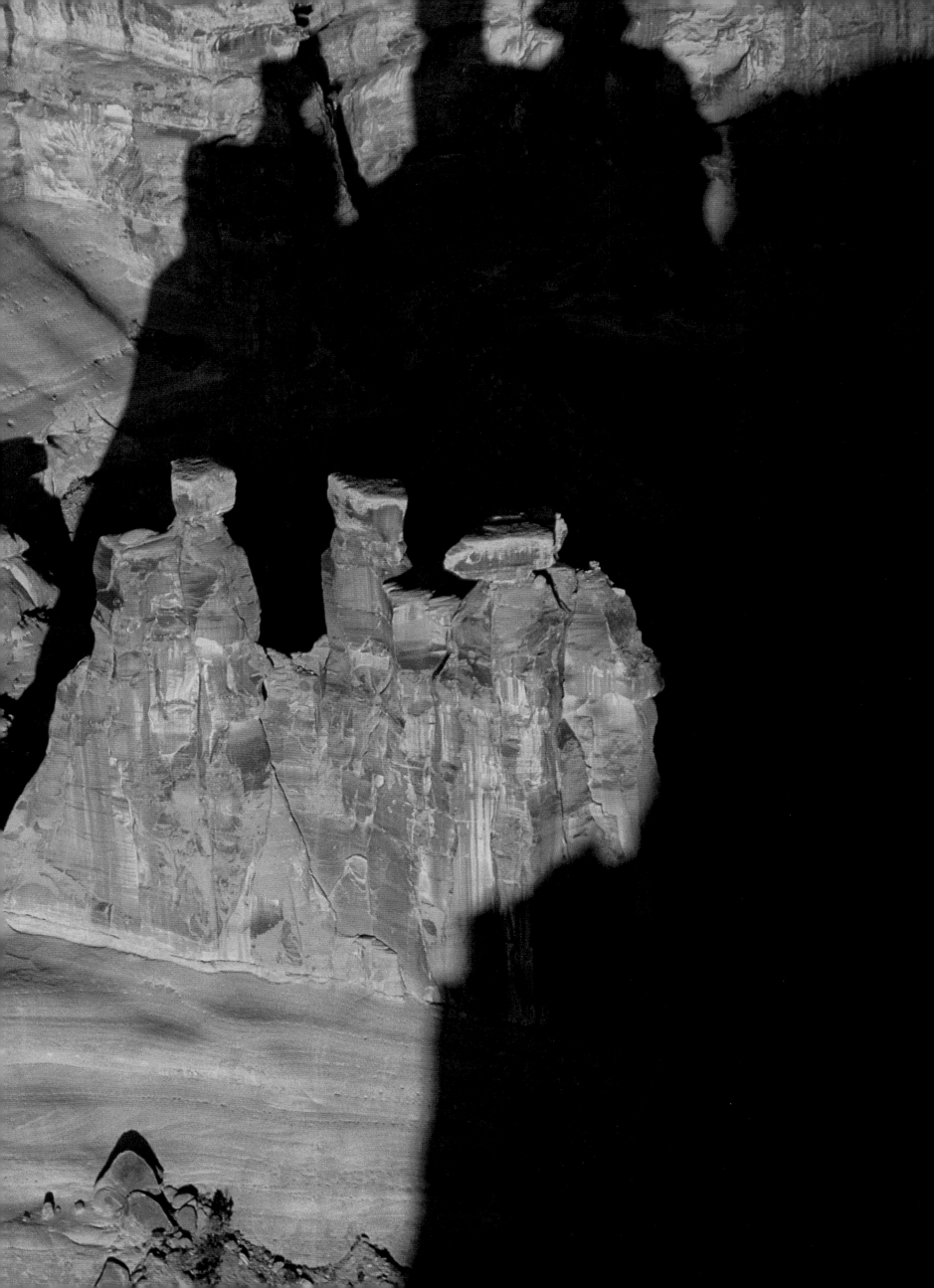

SACRED LANDS OF

Aerial Photographs by Harvey Lloyd

Foreword by Michael Fox
Design by Massimo Vignelli

THE SOUTHWEST

THE MONACELLI PRESS

The Colorado Plateau

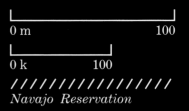

0 m   100

0 k   100

/////////////////
Navajo Reservation

*National Parks and Monuments
(NP, NM)*

Utah

Salt Lake City

Arches NP

Grand Junction

Moab

La Sal Mountains

Canyonlands NP

Colorado

Bryce Canyon NP

Monticello

Glen Canyon

Mexican Hat

Cortez

Lake Powell

Mesa Verde NP

Monument Valley

Page

El Capitan

Kayenta

Shiprock

Taos Pueblo

Painted Desert

*Chaco Canyon
National Historic Area*

Taos

Hopi Mesas

Grand Canyon NP

*Canyon de Chelly
NM*

Santa Fe

Wupatki NM

San Francisco Peaks

Sunset Crater NM

Gallup

Mount Taylor

Flagstaff

Albuquerque

Zuni

Grants

*Meteor
Crater*

Sedona

Petrified Forest NP

Acoma Pueblo

Arizona

New Mexico

Contents

For Shirlee and Andrei

Among the rarest and most resonant moments in history are those times when opposites converge to create something altogether new—when the right people somehow appear in the right place at just the right time to enact change that will affect the lives of succeeding generations long into the future.   —*Museum of Northern Arizona*

First published in the United States of America in 1995 by
The Monacelli Press, Inc.,
10 East 92nd Street, New York, New York 10128.

Library of Congress Cataloging-in-Publication Data
Lloyd, Harvey.
Sacred lands of the Southwest : aerial photographs / by Harvey Lloyd ; foreword by Michael Fox ; design by Massimo Vignelli ; with an anthology of writings by Native Americans and others.
p. cm.
Includes bibliographical references (p.).
ISBN 1-885254-11-3
1. Colorado Plateau—Aerial photographs. 2. National parks and reserves— Colorado Plateau—Aerial photographs. 3. Sacred space—Colorado Plateau— Aerial photographs. 4. Indians of North America—Colorado Plateau— Antiquities—Aerial photographs. I. Title.
F788.L75 1995
917.91'3'00222—dc20   95-30602

Page 224 constitutes an extension of this page.

Printed and bound in Hong Kong.

Pages 2–3: Church Rock, Red Rock State Park, New Mexico
Pages 4–5: Three Gossips, or Three Magi, Arches National Park, Utah
Pages 6–7: Castle Rock, Lake Powell/Glen Canyon, Page, Arizona
Pages 8–9: Sun Temple, Mesa Verde National Park, Colorado
Pages 10–11: Hopi Point, Grand Canyon, Arizona

Acknowledgments

I would like to thank the many people who participated in creating this volume:

The Native Americans who first settled this land and lived in harmony with the spirits, and their descendants. Their wisdom and love for the sacred earth and its creatures first made me aware of our vast indebtedness to these freedom-loving peoples.

My associate and loving friend of the keen and elegant eye, Shirlee Price, ever tenacious in her pursuit of excellence. This book could not have been made without Shirlee's good spirits, patience, and skill.

My gifted son Andrei Lloyd, my friend, counselor, and valued adviser.

My foresighted friend Michael Fox, who first gave me the opportunity to work with Native American cultures during production of *Our Voices, Our Land,* and the trustees and the staff of the Museum of Northern Arizona.

Gianfranco Monacelli and his committed crew: Andrea Monfried, Steve Sears, Julia Joern, and Monica Cavazzini.

Massimo Vignelli, gifted designer, and his talented associate, Rocco Piscatello.

Spencer Frazier, my friend, whose creativity, sensitivity, and drive gave me comfort during difficult assignments around the world.

My friend and counselor Joe Burke.

Kate Longbotham, friend and associate at our studio, whose hard work and pursuit of quality helped so much to make this book.

Elaine and Marty, Rachelle, Stephen, and Laurie, my good-spirited, talented, understanding, and warm-hearted family.

Sally Lloyd and Richard Steedman, lovers of fine photography.

William Martinez, artist and sculptor of Taos Pueblo, New Mexico.

The young and old pilots of Cessna 172s, 182s and 182RGs, 206s, and 210RGs: Bonnie Lindgren, Dale Ogden, Robert R. Lindgren, Gary Glodowski, and Beth Roy at Redtail Aviation of Moab; T. Jim Sheppard of Gallup Flying Services; Richard Payton, Kyle Howes, and Michael Jordan of Scenic Airlines in Page; Bill E. Yoder and Ethan Waybright of Alpine Air Service of Flagstaff; Larry Gordon at Grants; Ed Becvarik of Air West Aviation in Santa Fe; Ecki Anders of Zia Aviation in Santa Fe; Kevin Nessheim of Aerovision, Inc., in Sedona; Bill Moore of Cortez Flying Service, Inc.; Guy M. Bate of Air Taos; and Patrick Arthur Jones of Air Grand Canyon. Bravo and heartfelt thanks to these talented men and women—and their crews—whose eagerness and good fellowship made us welcome each new challenge while soaring over often hazardous and difficult terrain.

Deepak ("Baboo") Kumar, proprietor, Sheetal Kumar, Ahmad Riaz Hameed, Vikas Vats, and staff, Baboo Color Labs, New York; Juanita Hill, Steve Parker, Greg Calder, and staff, Stokes Imaging Service of Austin, Texas.

My very old friends at Professional Camera Repair Service in New York City, Rick Rankin, Herb Zimmerman, and staff.

The master builders of the gyro-stabilizer, my friend Henry Struck and the staff of Ken Labs, Essex, Connecticut. Without Henry's invisible tripod, this book would have foundered in unstable air.

The inns and hotels that gave us warm hospitality: Paul R. Bynum, Best Western Canyonlands, Moab, Utah; Sheryl Carrick, Best Western Grand Canyon Squire Inn, Arizona; Wahweap Lodge/Marina, Lake Powell, Page, Arizona; James J. Bagby, the Inn at Loretto, Santa Fe, New Mexico; Steven Klein, Woodlands Plaza Hotel, Flagstaff, Arizona; the Historic Taos Inn, New Mexico; Holiday Inn of Gallup, New Mexico. A comfortable room, an excellent ambience, and a fine meal after a day in the air are paradise enough.

Foreword
Michael Fox, Director, Museum of Northern Arizona and Harold S. Colton Research Center, Flagstaff, Arizona

In *Sacred Lands of the Southwest*, my friend Harvey Lloyd's photographs portray why we celebrate the Colorado Plateau. The land enchants us and we wish to know and understand it. Perhaps the humans who are allowed to know it best are the Native Americans who have coursed the land for millennia and left traces of their heritage in magnificent cliff dwellings and pueblos. Quests by explorers and scientists in the name of intelligence have perused most of the plateau's mesas and inner canyons and examined the geologic past and present. Because we find this land so fascinating, we want to investigate every inch of it. Yet even with this fervent examination, a few cultural secrets and a few remote canyons still remain unknown to the prying eyes of modern society. May these mysteries endure.

Once we intrude, we feel we must gain mastery and so we aim to tame this land with dams, roads, and other temporary encumbrances, all the while humbly acknowledging that our impact is only momentary. We like to believe our constructed edifices create permanent change, but it is the plateau that truly represents permanence. The vast canyons, rock configurations, and reminders of ancient civilizations often appear to be unchanging—after all, it took millions of years to create the images we enjoy on these pages.

What does change frequently on the Colorado Plateau is the weather, and this characteristic molds the terrain. The adage "If you don't like the weather, wait an hour" is applicable to the plateau. Weather quickly changes from calm to storm, clear to clouds, dry to wet, and then back again. A quiet walk on the south rim of the Grand Canyon begins on a calm, sunny morning, and by the end of the walk, an east wind blows fiercely enough to make you hold onto your hat.

Some call the Colorado Plateau inhospitable with its extreme weather: aridity or flash floods, intense cold or heat, gale winds or suffocating stillness. Others call it magical and alluring with side canyons bursting with

16

tropical plants and wildflowers. Fortunate foresight in the form of national parks and monuments has protected many of the stark landforms pictured here. People flock to the area to visit the landscape to try, at least for a moment, to taste the timeless feeling of the plateau. Harvey's camera captures these feelings and then liberates them for us to savor. The dramatic aerial images distinctly display the plateau in its glory, influenced, as always, by weather.

My work with Harvey on *Our Voices, Our Land* tells me he grasps the essence of the plateau. He is now developing a multimedia presentation on natural and human historic images of the Colorado Plateau that will introduce visitors to the Museum of Northern Arizona, which has long observed and honored the people and places of the region.

Sacred Lands of the Southwest reveals why natives and non-natives consider the land blessed. This book is a warm and exceptional tribute to a region we respect and love. May your enjoyment of it give you the peaceful and graceful feeling that you are soaring like an eagle over the Colorado Plateau.

Prologue
Harvey Lloyd

The world before me is restored in hozhó
The world behind me is restored in hozhó
The world below me is restored in hozhó
The world above me is restored in hozhó
All things around me are restored in hozhó
My voice is restored in hozhó
It is finished in hozhó
It is finished in hozhó
It is finished in hozhó
It is finished in hozhó.
—Ron McCoy

Hozhó . . . the word means something like harmony, beauty, and balance all wrapped in one concept that dwells at the heart of the Navajo world view. —Paul G. Zolbrod

To fly over these lands, as I have flown over these lands, to ride these ancient corridors of air and time, creates a resonance, bestirs a sacred music that strums my heart strings, plays on my soul like a double bass, singing, murmuring, bellowing, whispering a joyful chorale as old as creation. I hear the bass chant of early plainsong rising like distant thunder over the stone canyons and the sacred peaks. I witness celestial melodies rain down like bright plumed arrows from the Milky Way, fiery in the desert night. I see myriad stone cathedrals, towers of blazing light and iron oxide, rust red, burnt orange, and sulphur yellow in the desert sunsets. I smell the sage and the juniper. Just before sunset, crepuscular shadows stalk the land like prancing wild horses, and hooves of darkness pummel the pitted desert floor. At dawn, a pale full moon trembles before the cymbal clash of sunrise. Each day is sacred, each day cocooned in wonder.

I call these lands sacred lands because they are sacred to Native Americans and to those who came before: the Anasazi, the ancient ones. I call these lands sacred lands because they are sacred to all Americans who view nature's handiwork, our heritage, with pride, wonder, and respect.

It is like this; as long as you stay within the realm of the great Cloudbeings, you may indeed walk at the very edge of the Deep Canyon and not be harmed. You will be protected by the rainbow and by the Great Ones . . . —Tewa man

The inexorable grip of nature's harsh hand defends much of the Colorado Plateau desert lands. The plateau straddles parts of Arizona, New Mexico, Utah, and Colorado like an eagle's wings bright with sacred feathers, a war bonnet, a mantle made of etherial spirits. Only such formidable desert landscapes, dry and barren, rock ribbed and buttressed like a crusader fortress, trenched, canyoned, and crevassed, studded with stone guardians, goblins, and totems, can survive the onrush of careless development.

No, this land is no desert. It is ancient Eden, sanctified and resurrected in beauty. It is the land of Kokopelli, humpbacked flute player, coyote the trickster, and Wakan Tanka, maker and guardian of the earth. These parks, monuments, tribal lands, and ruins trumpet a triumphant music, hosanna on the highest.

The primeval muse and mystery of the Southwest appears like fog and haze over the canyons during a thunderstorm, pale, ephemeral, crooning of turquoise and silver, golden corn and the rainbows of silence and solitude. When your heart flowers with sage, poppies, chokecherry, and pale-gold cruciferae, your soul whistles in the dry wind and you shed all doubts. The desert comes alive. Sacred spirits appear, dancing, trailing remnants of glory. Ghost dancers flaunt golden curtains of rain that hang and drift over the gorges and canyons of the Colorado Plateau at sunset. You smile and witness . . .

A cross section of the North American craton, if one were available, would reveal the geological history of the continent back to Precambrian times. There is only one place where part of such a cross section can be seen . . . the Colorado Plateau . . . the mainstream, the Colorado River, cut so deeply into the plateau that the basement rocks themselves have been revealed . . . the plateau and its canyons have added immeasurable to understanding of the geological and evolutionary story of the last 570 million years . . . During this period life on Earth progressed from trilobite to man . . . —Ron Redfern

As part of a public proclamation of Native American attitudes, a group of Hopi religious leaders said, "The land is like the sacred inner chamber of a church—our Jerusalem." It is my Jerusalem as well.

Oh my desert Jerusalem, you display your stone amphitheaters, your rock-buttressed cathedrals, your rugged, timeless vistas. Your lucid air glows pale blue in the haze of dawn, saffron, pink, and gold after the thunderstorms. Your thick hide is cracked, fissured like an old elephant's skin brown and muddy after bathing, crenelated and peaked, pyramided and snow clad, rainbowed with the light of the clear desert air. Your red, yellow, and umber rocks parade in ranks, arrayed like monumental chess sets. Your land is studded with stone arches and bridges rudely carved like a Titan's sculpture; it is an archetypal landscape from the dawn of creation, resplendent, stupendous, sacred, with holy sites, tabernacles, and temples built on stone foundations two billion years old—the basilica, the royal house of the Colorado Plateau.

Sun is our father. He knows each one of us and when the first light shines upon the earth, He is making a count of His children. If you are awake and standing, you are counted as being alive. But if Sun peers inside your hogan and finds you lying down asleep, you are counted as being dead. —Cecilia Etcitty

Here we encounter a landscape of ancient dreams and holy visions, the mysteries told by shamans, prophets, and medicine men, the whispers of the great owl at night, the hoarse cries of the eagle suspended high over the sacred peaks, the coarse coughs of coyote— the origins of myths amid shining fields of maize and desert gold flowers.

Given wings of aluminum and an eye of glass,
I fix this realm of myth and grandeur and
bring it down to earth, to common ground.

You look at that mountain.
There's a quiet there
and yet there's a fervor there.
And if you've ever seen clouds there
you see that mountain
like a hand grasping those clouds.
There's like a handshake between the Earth
and Father Sky. —Navajo man

During these journeys I encountered
shamans, eagles, ghost dancers, reborn
spirits, wrestling with and enduring powerful
forces tens of millions of years old above the
Colorado Plateau, the high windy mesas, and
the thin dry envelope of air over the plateau,
dry washes, and cleft canyons and the grand
and desolate ruins of the Anasazi. I was
racked, crushed, and broken by ancient
memories, keel-hauled on the stone wheel of
the desert, clasped and bloodied by iron
maidens of granite cruciforms and spires of
stone, the sacred lands, and I was always
joyful and content with the knowledge that
the gods and spirits were merciful.

We are the Stars which sing.
We sing with our light;
We are the birds of fire,
We fly over the sky
Our light is a voice;
We make a road
For the spirit to pass over.
—Algonquian

What is sacred? I fly over Monument Valley
at sunset. Yei Bi Chei Rocks, Totem Pole, Big
Indian, King on his Throne, West Mitten, and
Stagecoach stretch long shadows into the
dusk. Swaths of dark green stripe the desert
floor. I whirl and plunge, stoop and dive like a
falcon or an eagle hungry for prey. The
aircraft tumbles through the air. Stall
warnings squeal. Flaps up. Flaps down.
Gear up. Gear down. The monuments parade
below, transubstantial choirs silent, immense,
eternal. Shadows lengthen and march to the
reddening horizon. Fire, translucent red fire,
like the effluence of ghosts, flares on the

Opposite: Balanced Rock,
Arches National Park, Utah
Pages 20–21:
Eagle Cloud, Utah
Pages 24–25:
Canyon de Chelly, Arizona
Pages 28–29:
Sunset Crater, Arizona

towers. Suddenly, darkness. Who watches in the night?

The life of these Indians is nothing but a continuous religious experience . . . To them, the essence of religion is . . . the "spirit of wonder" . . . the recognition of life as power, as a mysterious, [ever-present] concentrated form of non-material energy, of something loose about the world and contained in a more or less condensed degree by every object. —de Angulo

Terry Tempest Williams has described the Southwest and its sacred places and peoples in her books Pieces of White Shell *and* Coyote's Canyon. *The following excerpts from her books describe in meaningful terms the area that means so much to me.*

This is Coyote's country—a landscape of the imagination, where nothing is as it appears. The buttes, mesas, and red rock spires beckon you to see them as something else: cathedrals, tabletops, bear's ears, nuns. Window and arches ask you to recall what is no longer there, to taste the wind for the sandstone it carries. These astonishing formations invite a new mythology for desert goers, one that acknowledges the power of story and ritual yet lies within the integrity of our own cultures.

Coyote knows we do not matter. He knows rocks care nothing for those who wander through them; and yet he also knows that those same individuals who care for rocks will find openings—large openings—that become passageways into the unseen world, where music is heard through dove's wings and wisdom is gleaned from the tails of lizards. Coyote is always nearby, but remains hidden. He is an ally because he cares enough to stay wary. He teaches us how to survive.

That night I made my bed on a slab of slickrock. I spent an eerie night among nocturnal cries and shrieks . . . Were these allies of Coyote? . . . Then, coming up from the Hovenweep ruins, I heard drums.

Boom-ba-boom, boom, boom. Boom-ba-boom, boom, boom . . . Anasazi Drums. They continued until the sun rose. Boom-ba-boom, boom . . . Then silence. Nothing. No sound. No movement. Nothing.

For some time now, I have tried to explain rationally where these nocturnal beats originated, but to no avail. River cobbles? No river. A powwow? No people for miles around. As a last resort, I approached an old Native American woman who was the grandmother of a child I was teaching. I explained the sounds and the circumstances to her, and she smiled and said, "You heard what you heard."

The next morning I hiked out of the canyon alone. In the middle of the trail lay a fresh pile of Coyote dung. A golden scarab crawled out.

Silence. That is time you are hearing. We are in Anasazi country. This is a place where canyon walls rise upward like praying hands. Veins of water run between them. You may choose to walk here, ankle deep in the midst of chubs and minnows. If you wish you can brace your hands flush against either side of the slickrock and fancy yourself pushing down walls. Look up. the sky is a blue ribbon. These are the canyons, cool refuges from exposed heat, dripping with red mimulus and ferns. This is the landscape that gave these people birth . . .

You cannot travel very long through Navajoland without stubbing your toe on the Anasazi.

Geologically speaking, Navajoland lies within the Colorado Plateau. The Colorado Plateau is characterized by horizontal, sedimentary formations, deeply incised drainage systems, aridity, and sparse vegetation. It is a physiographic province bordered by the Great Basin to the west and the Rocky Mountains to the north and east.

A man traveled through this country with a bag of corn seed over one shoulder. His shadow against the desert looked like a deformity. He would stop at every village and teach the people how to plant corn. And then when the sun slipped behind the mesa and the village was asleep, he would walk through the cornfields playing his flute. The seeds would flower, pushing themselves up through the red, sandy soil and follow the high-pitched notes upward. The sun would rise and the man would be gone, with corn stalks the height of a young girl shimmering in the morning light. Many of the young women would complain of a fullness in their bellies. The elders would smile, knowing they were pregnant. They would look southward and call him "Kokopelli."

During the Paleozoic era, about 600 million years ago, this land was periodically covered by shallow seas. The shoreline migrated west, exposing broad tracts of ancient seabeds. These earliest rocks are exposed only in the deepest canyons.

Pieces of white shell. I would never think of associating these gifts from the ocean with the desert. But then, I am not Navajo. My knowledge of earth is literal, with distinct categories and fixed points. I have always been told you find seashells on the beach, pinecones in the forest, and bleached bones on the desert. I have believed in predictabilities, but should I wander awhile? Remove myself from asphalt paths. Take off my shoes. Unbraid my hair. Forget biological rules and constraints. Then could I see Pacific waves roll in, carrying pinecones from the sea? Or dream of fragile, fertile possibilities—of seashells dangling from the boughs of lodgepole pines? Perhaps even expect to see bare, bleached bones resume their stance in life? Pieces of white shell in the desert? White shell, the currency between cultures.

During the Mesozoic era, 225 million to 70 million years ago, the scene changed dramatically. The seas retreated again and an interior basin was created due to the rise of the Mesocordilleran High on one side and the ancestral Rocky Mountains on the other. At this time, non-marine deposits were laid by wind and water. Evidence of this process can be found in Navajo sandstone which once stood as dunes, Kayenta and Moenave formations which were once stream deposits, and the Chinle formation which speaks of both lake and stream deposits with traces of volcanic ash. These formations were laid in the Triassic period.

The Navajo identify four sacred mountains which border the reservation today. They all have mythical origins.

These mountains have been set up as our, our Constitution. Yes, it is like the very same thing which the white people call their Constitution. For us these four mountains were set up and sanctified for that same purpose.

These mountains include Blanca Peak, or Sis Naajiní, located on the eastern border of Navajoland. First Man and First Woman fastened Sis Naajiní to the earth with a bolt of white lightning.

They covered the mountain with a blanket of daylight, and they decorated it with white shells, white lightning, black clouds, and male rain. They placed the white shell basket on the summit, and in this basket two eggs of the pigeons. They said that the pigeons were to be the mountain's feather. And they sent Bear to guard the doorway of White Bead Boy in the east.

Mt. Taylor, Tso dzil, is located in the south. Here, it is said, First Man and First Woman fastened the mountain to earth with a stone knife.

They covered this mountain of the south with a blue cloud blanket; and they decorated it with turquoise, white corn, dark mists, and female rain. They placed a turquoise basket on the highest peak, and in it they put two eggs of the Bluebird. Bluebirds are Tso dzil's feathers. They sent Big Snake to guard the doorway of Turquoise Boy in the south.

The mountain guarding the west is San Francisco Peak, Dook'o'oosłííd to the west, where it was fastened to earth with a sunbeam.

First Man and First Woman covered the mountain of the west with a yellow cloud. They adorned it with haliotis shell, yellow corn, black clouds, and the male rain, and they called many animals to dwell upon it. They placed the abalone shell basket on the summit, and in it they placed the two eggs of yellow warbler. These birds were to become its feathers. Black Wind was told to go to the west and guard the doorway of Abalone Shell Boy.

Hesperus Peak, Dibéntsáá, is the sacred mountain to the north. It was fastened by First Man and First Woman to earth by a rainbow.

Over it they spread a blanket of darkness. They decorated it with obsidian, black vapors, and different plants and animals. The basket they placed on its highest peak was of obsidian, and in it they put two eggs of blackbird. The blackbirds are the mountain's feathers. Lightning was sent to guard Jet Boy's doorway in the north.

During the late Jurassic, a brief incursion from the north took place as a narrow seaway flowed through. The deposits from the sea produced the Carmel and Twin Creeks formations. Finally, seas flooded the Colorado Plateau once again, ending the Cretaceous period of the Mesozoic era. Imagine coal forming lagoons and bayous along the shoreline—the transformation today being the Kaiparowitz Plateau and mancos shale.

Chaco Canyon. The standing ruins have metamorphosed into standing rocks. From the sun-scorched earth they were taken, to the same soil they return. The cool breezes which run through them are the voice and spirit of Anasazi . . .

Before leaving Chaco, I step inside a small pueblo room. I don't think anyone saw me; for some reason this is important. Solitude. Whitewashed walls. Hand prints, streaked across the surface. Female energy. I hold my hand against hers. Cold contact. Her hand, so much smaller, more square. I shiver. I picture a young woman sitting in the corner, legs outstretched—perhaps a babe at her breast. Silence. I don't want there to be: Silence. I want to talk, listen, share, spend entire afternoons in womanly conversation about her life, mine. Somehow, I sense that a thousand years do not separate us.

In the Cenozoic era, the seas were expelled as North America was uplifted. Superimposed on this continental uplift were numerous local areas of more dramatic crustal activity: areas such as the Uinta Mountains, the San Rafael Swell, the Uncompahgre, the Kaibab Plateau, and the Monument Upwarp. It is referred to by geologists as the "Laramide Orogeny," which took place sometime between 60 and 40 million years ago. This was the beginning of the modern topography of the Colorado Plateau as we know it.

If you sit on the canyon's edge, looking down, you watch the end of a day. This is the place where tall shadows dwell. They stretch across the land, their heads towering over me. When they arrived, I am not certain. How they move about in such stillness, only the Sun could betray their secret . . .

An evening primrose blooms and then another. I hold out my hands and make bird shadows on the sandstone. I hear the whistling of dove flight and the song of canyon wren. Violet-green swallows, white-throated swifts, and nighthawks wing their way through rock mazes and circle first stars. I watch vultures soar and see clay-colored mammals traverse the flats. My feet are startled by the black-and-white flickerings of King Snake. I look across— only a few seconds of sunset remain . . .

Who knows about this desert? I may be here for days. Perhaps I shall be an arch tomorrow.

Also during this time, lakes began to develop in the lowlands between uplifts. Watersheds were created. The Claron formation of Bryce Canyon and the Green River formation are testimonials to these past lakebeds.

One night the stars pulled me into a dream. A basket sat before me, coiled: around and around and around and around. It was striped with persimmon. I should not touch it. This much I knew. I knelt down closely and saw a woman's long black hair curled between stitches. I picked up a sprig of salt bush and rattled it above the hair strand. Suddenly, the woven bowl began to pulsate, writhe, until a snake uncoiled herself slowly. This is what I heard:

Sha-woman, Sha-woman, hiss
Sha-woman, Sha-woman, hiss
Tongue, rattle, hiss
Tongue, rattle, hiss
Sha-woman, Sha-woman, hiss.

She stopped. She raised her head and blew upward. I watched the breezes pull her vertically until she became a white desert torch.

As surface upheavals continued, an intense downcutting of streams and an integration of drainages took place. This action is largely responsible for the development of the spectacular canyons associated with the Southwest. The law of uniformitarianism tells us that what happened then is still happening today. What is left of the Colorado River continues to cut.

I was walking down a dirt road in Chinle, Arizona. It was well after dusk. An old man approached. We stopped and talked. We listened to each other celebrate the night, as the Big Dipper rested on the western horizon.

"You know the Milky Way is the path of souls . . ." he said.

A crescent moon hung over a hogan and the stars seemed especially bright . . . I thought about what the old man had just said so casually. I looked up to the sky once again. The Pleiades were as they had always been.

Volcanic rocks spewn across the Colorado Plateau are reminiscent of eruptions during late Cenozoic time. Shallow intrusions of magma slowly worked their way to the surface, appearing as blisters rather than explosions due to the thickness of the earth's crust. The Henry, La Sal, and Abajo mountains are all examples of this process. They have been raised by an igneous fist. Remnants of true volcanic eruptions are Agatha Peak, the Hopi diatremes, and Shiprock. Standing as black spires, they are the throats of volcanoes.

There is a phrase spoken by the Navajo— *Sa'ah naagháii bik'eh hozhó*—which roughly translates into their expression of happiness, health, the beauty of earth, and the harmony of their relations with others. *Sa'ah naagháii* represents the capacity of all life and living things to achieve immortality through reproduction or perpetuation of the species. *Sa'ah* denotes the verb usage "to grow, or mature." The propagation of the Navajo People is founded upon growth, or emergence from four preceding worlds, each evolution shedding darkness and gaining more light and refinement, thus enabling them to come closer to the universal whole, to beauty or hozhó. *Bik'eh hozhó* represents the peace and harmony essential to the perpetuation of all living species.

At the east the rainbow
dawn maidens with sh...
and shirts of yellow da...
Beautifully over us it is...
Above us on the mount...
I go around the fruits a...
shimmer. Above us amo...
the shimmering fruits ...
shirts of yellow are ben...
On the beautiful mount...
it is daylight. —Mescale...

moves forward,

nmering shoes

ce over us.

dawning . . .

ins, with shoes of yellow

d the herbs that

ng the mountains,

ith shoes and

towards him.

in above,

ro Apache Ceremony

Grand Canyon

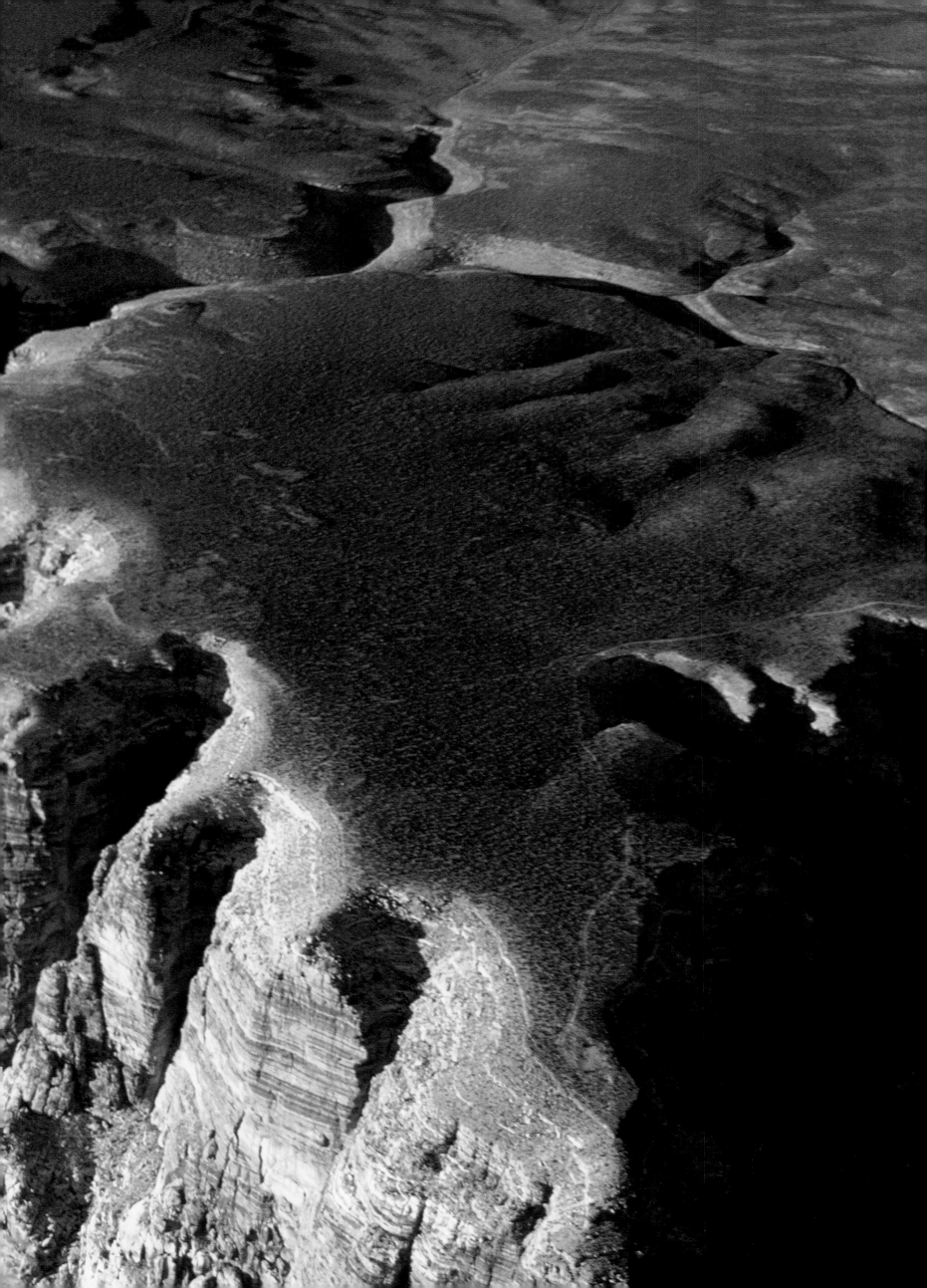

One might imagine this was intended for the library of the gods; and so it was. The shelves are not for books, but form the stony leaves of one great book. He who would read the language of the universe may dig out letters here and there, and with them spell words, and read, in a slow and imperfect way, but still so as to understand a little, the story of creation. —*John Wesley Powell*

The Grand Canyon of the Colorado is a great innovation in modern ideas of scenery, and in our conceptions of the grandeur, beauty, and power of nature. As with all great innovations it is not to be comprehended in a day or a week, nor even in a month. It must be dwelt upon and studied, and the study must comprise the slow acquisition of the meaning and spirit of that marvelous scenery which characterizes the Plateau country, and of which the great chasm is the superlative manifestation.
—*Clarence E. Dutton*

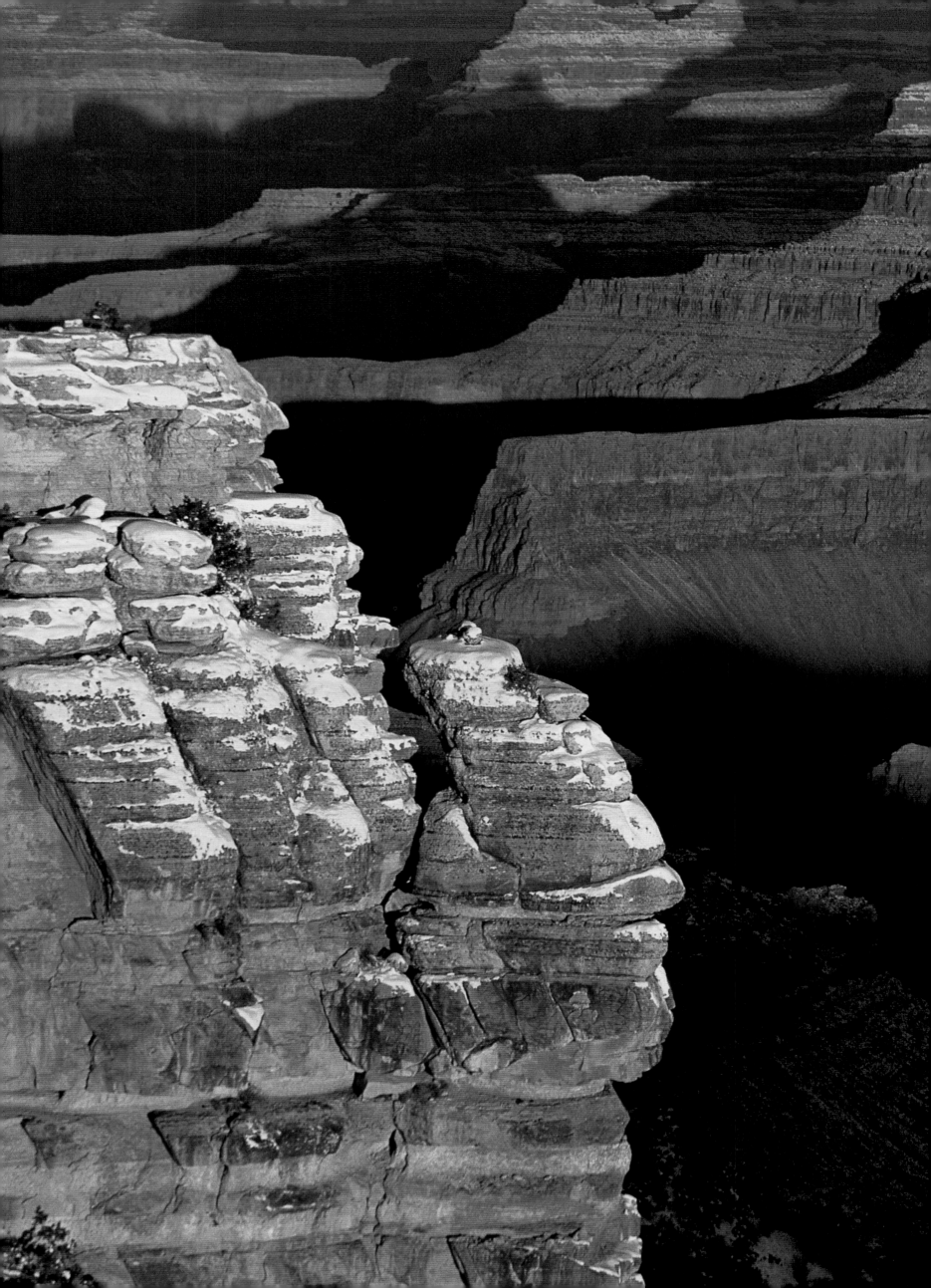

I focus quietly each day on the stone, the breathing of time locked up here, back to the Proterozoic, before there were sea shells. Look up to wisps of high cirrus overhead, the hint of a mare's tail sky. Close my eyes: tappet of water against the boat, sound of an Anasazi's six-hole flute . . . The canyon seems like a grandfather . . . [There is a] moment of fumbling awe one feels on first seeing the Brahma schist at the dead bottom of the canyon's Inner Gorge. Your fingertips graze the 1.9-billion-year-old stone as the boat drifts slowly past. With the loss of self-consciousness, the landscape opens . . . Each day we are upended, if not by some element of the landscape itself then by what the landscape does, visibly, to each of us. It has snapped us like fresh-laundered sheets . . . Each evening we enjoy a vespers: cicadas and crickets, mourning doves, vermillion flycatchers. And the wind, for which chimes are hung in a salt cedar. Those notes leap above the splash and rattle, the grinding of water and the roar of rapids . . . From the rims the canyon seems oceanic; at the surface of the river the feeling is intimate . . . It is this known dimension of distance and time and the perplexing question posed by the canyon itself—What is consequential?—that reverberate constantly . . . A thought that stayed with me was that I had entered a private place in the earth. I had seen exposed nearly its oldest part. I had lost my sense of urgency, rekindled a sense of what people were . . . Two kinds of time pass here: sitting at the edge of a sun-warmed pool watching blue dragonflies and black tadpoles. And the rapids: down the glassy-smooth tongue into a yawing trench, climb a ten-foot wall of standing water and fall into boiling, ferocious hydraulics, sucking whirlpools, drowned voices, stopped hearts . . . I do not know, really, how we will survive without places like the Inner Gorge of the Grand Canyon to visit. Once in a lifetime, even, is enough. To feel the stripping down, an ebb of the press of conventional time, a radical change of proportion, an unspoken respect for others that elicits keen emotional pleasure, a quick, intimate pounding of the heart. Some parts of the trip will emerge one day . . . in a gesture of friendship to some stranger . . . in a note of gratitude to nameless faces in the Park Service, in wondering . . . The living of life, any life, involves great and private pain, much of which we share with no one. In such places as the Inner Gorge the pain trails away from us. It is not so quiet there or so removed that you can hear yourself think, that you would even wish to; that comes later. You can hear your heart beat. That comes first. —*Barry Lopez*

Imagine for a moment, how the Amerindian peoples experienced the world before the coming of white people. A generation of people would come and go, and come again on the earth, like the grass or the buffalo or the leaves on the trees—and earth remained the same . . . To die in such a world is no great tragedy: the seasons turn; the spiral comes around again; the eternal is everywhere present . . . The turning cycles of time wheel on, reflecting the eternal light of which they are the manifestation and in which we live, whether we know it or not.
—*Arthur Versluis*

Then weave for us a garm

May the warp be the whit

May the weft be the red li

May the fringes be the fal

May the border be the sta

That we may walk fitting

That we may walk fitting

Oh our Mother the Earth,

—Songs of the Tewa

ent of brightness;

light of morning,

t of evening,

ng rain,

ding rainbow,

y where the birds sing,

y where the grass is green,

Oh our Father the Sky.

Sacred Mountains

This page: Navajo
Mountain, Lake Powell/
Glen Canyon, Arizona
Opposite and overleaf:
San Francisco Peaks,
Flagstaff, Arizona

Preceding pages:
Mount Taylor, New Mexico

55

Sometimes I dream thi[s]
its overhanging walls, [w]
with cattail, sweet clove[r]
over cutbanks of red-ta[n]
azure with grosbeaks. I[t]
everywhere. Fragrant r[...]
slapping into water beh[ind]
of muskrat and raccoo[n]
the beasts themselves lo[...]
dreamed. —Ann Weiler

incipient lake and

s sandbars pungent

 with willow bending

gled roots and flashing

timations are

ck, beveled sandbanks

nd our backs, tracks

slicked on algaed clay,

g vanished or only

Walka

Glen Canyon/Lake Powell

Entering through a little grove of box-elder and cottonwood trees, we find ourselves in a vast chamber carved out of rock. At the upper end there is a clear, deep pool of water, bordered with verdure . . . Through the ceiling and on through the rocks for a thousand feet above, there is a narrow, winding skylight, and this is all carved out by a little stream which runs only during the few showers that fall now and then in this arid country . . . When "Old Shady" sings us a song at night, we are pleased to find that this hollow in the rock is filled with sweet sounds. It was doubtless made for an academy of music by its storm-born architect; so we name it Music Temple. —*John Welsey Powell*

Is it not of great significance that the world of stars permeates all movements of water, that water infuses all earthly life with the events of the cosmos, that all life processes are through water intimately connected with the course of the stars? . . . Thus water becomes an image of the stream of time itself, permeated with the rhythms of the starry world. All the creatures of the earth live in this stream of time, it flows within them, and, as long as it flows, sustains them in the stream of life. —*Theodore Schwenk*

Now this is the day.
Our child.
Into the daylight
You will go out standin;
Reaching to the road of
When your road is fulfi
In your thought may w
To this end:
May you help us all to f
—Zuni

. . .

our sun father.

ed

live . . .

nish our roads.

Bryce Canyon

The verbal tradition . . . has suffered a
deterioration in time. What remains is
fragmentary; mythology, legend, lore . . .
and of course the idea itself, as crucial and
complete as it ever was. That is the miracle . . .
It is made with the whole memory, that
experience of the mind which is legendary as
well as historical, personal as well as cultural
. . . an evocation of three things in particular:
a landscape that is incomparable, a time that
is gone forever, and the human spirit, which
endures. —*N. Scott Momaday*

Behold! The mountain
The valley is sacred. Be
Behold! The canyon is s
is sacred. I climb on the
valley. I wade in the riv
The sky is my pillow. B
my father. Behold! The
Behold! The river is my
The canyon is my broth
an eagle. I, I am the mo
valley. I, I am the river.
I, I am the sky.

s sacred. Behold!

old! The river is sacred.

acred. Behold! The sky

mountain. I walk in the

r. I walk in the canyon.

hold! The mountain is

alley is my mother.

sister. Behold!

r. Behold! The sky is

ntain. I, I am the

, I am the canyon.

Canyonlands

84

88

Listen to the air.
You can hear it, feel it,
smell it, taste it.
Woniya wakan, the hol[y]
which renews all by its
A good way to start thi[n]
talk about it.
Rather, talk to it,
talk to the rivers, the la[n]
to the winds,
as to our relatives.
—John Lame Deer

air,

reath . . .

king about nature,

es,

Life dances
in the womb
of our village.
Spirits of long ago
sing on purified sand.
The songs of beauty and life
seep down into the earth.
Rattling down the rain,
they sing of happiness.
Gourds of thunder
rumble under the song.
They dance one final prayer.
It is time for the last song.
Somewhere far away
Spruce Tree People
listen for rain songs.
Somewhere far away,
white clouds and rainbows
listen for one final prayer.
And here,
people of the fourth world
listen for the last song.
It is here
that we part with the breaking of branches.
—*Ransom Lomatewama*

Opposite: Sun Temple
Preceding pages:
Square Tower House
Overleaf: Cliff Palace
Second overleaf:
Oak Tree House

Oh, Male God! . . . With
made of the she-rain ou
us soaring. With the zig
out on high over your h
soaring. With the rainb
your head, come to us s
darkness made of the da
your wings, come to us
darkness on the earth,
—Washington Matthe

he far darkness

r your head, come to

ag lightning flung

ad, come to us

w hanging high over

aring. With the far

rk cloud on the ends of

oaring . . . With the

ome to us.

s

Shiprock

A voice said: "Grandson, what are you doing here?" Young Man turned and looked into the face of Man of Dark Color.

"I have come far," he answered, "from the country of the Utes. I am trying to reach my home, but the river is high and I cannot cross."

"Shall I take you across?" said Man of Dark Color. Young Man climbed on his back. When the two had crossed the San Juan River safely and Young Man had been put down gently, Man of Dark Color turned into a black rock that grew and grew, while his arms spread out into great wings.
He is there to this day: The Rock with Wings, Shiprock. —*Gerald Hausman*

It is lovely indeed, it is [
the spirit within the ear[
are my feet, The legs of [
The bodily strength of t[
strength, The thoughts [
thoughts, The voice of th[
The feather of the earth[
All that belongs to the e[
All that surrounds the [
I, I am the sacred word[
It is lovely indeed, it is [
—Navajo

ovely indeed. I, I am

th, The feet of the earth

he earth are my legs,

e earth is my bodily

f the earth are my

e earth is my voice,

s my feather,

rth belongs to me . . .

arth surrounds me . . .

of the earth,

ovely indeed.

Arches

More than 1,800 stone arches stand in Arches National Park . . . The stone sculpture and arches in the park represent 200 million years of geology. The entire park rests on a bed of salt in places a mile thick, the remains of an ancient sea that came and went in the Paradox Basin leaving behind layers of salt. Eventually, over millions of years, the salt bed was covered with thousands of feet of rocky debris washed down from the nearby mountains.

The mystery of the genesis of the arches and other rock formations in the park took place over a span of 150 million years. The mile-thick layer of salt under the immense weight of the overburden became malleable. The salt flowed like a glacier towards the southwest, buckling the layers of rock . . .

During the last ten million years, erosion removed rock deposits roughly a mile thick on top of the scenery. The relatively older Entrada Sandstone, formed over 140 million years ago, was exposed. Its erosion led to the creation of the extraordinary rock sculpture and arches. —*David W. Johnson*

This page and opposite:
Three Gossips, or Three Magi

The caprices of light, heat, and dust control the appearances. Sometimes the sky at dawn is as pallid as a snowdrop with pearly grays just emerging from the blue; and again it may be flushed with saffron, rose, and pink. When there are clouds and great heat the effect is often very brilliant. The colors are intense in chrome-yellows, golds, carmines, magentas, malachite-greens—a body of gorgeous hues upheld by enormous side wings of paler tints that encircle the horizon to the north and south, and send waves of color far up the sky to the cool zenith . . . The prevailing note of the sky, the one oftenest seen, is, of course, blue . . . There is no tale or testimony to be tortured out of the blue sky. It is a splendid body of color, no more. —*John C. Van Dyke*

In the Desert . . . the very fauna and flora proclaim that one can have a great deal of certain things while having very little of others; that one kind of scarcity is compatible with, perhaps even a necessary condition of, another kind of plenty—for instance, on even the level of things tangible or visible, that plenty of light and plenty of space may go with a scarcity of water . . .
—*Joseph Wood Krutch*

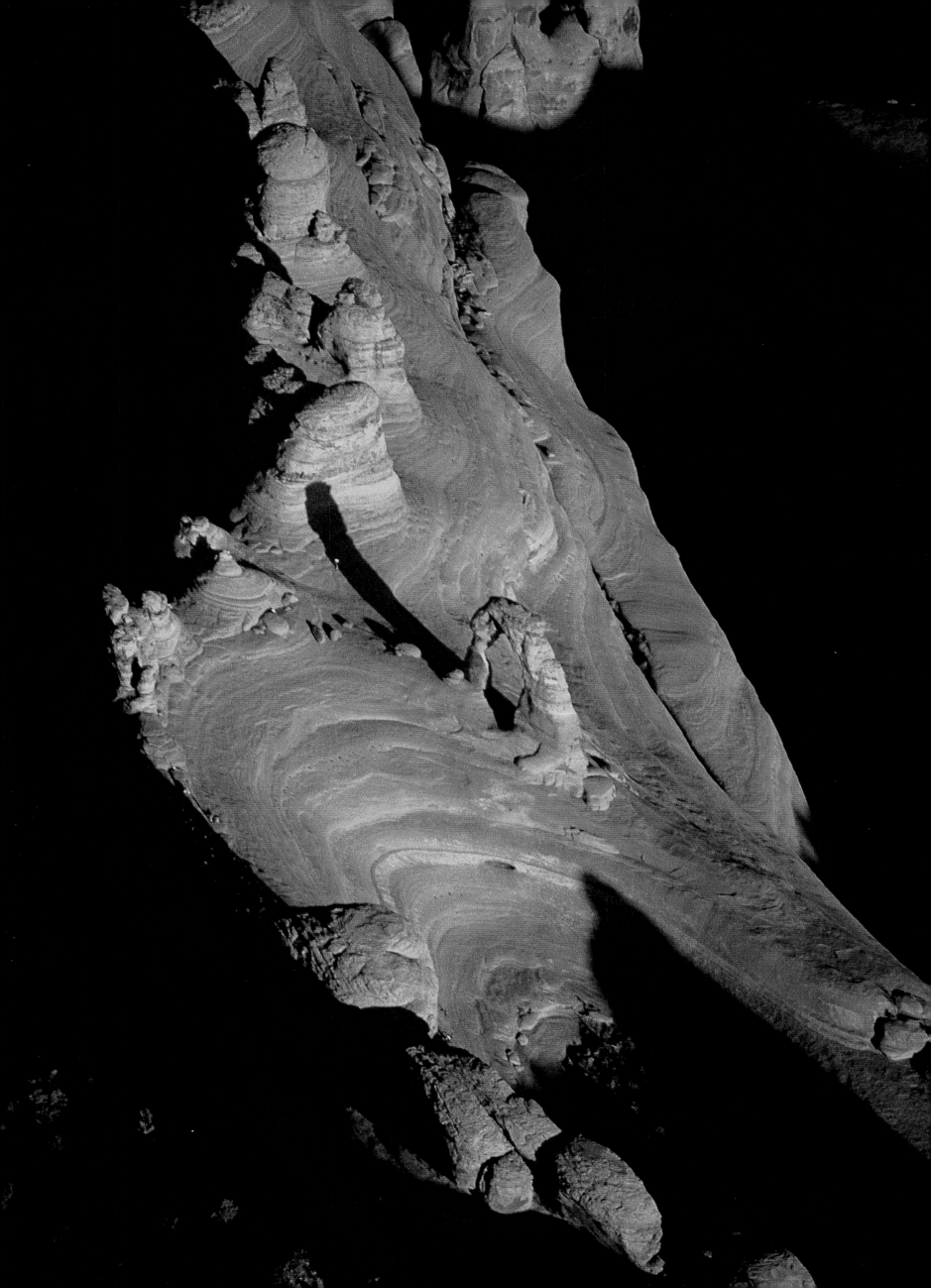

Where a stranger to the
perceive only the barren
perhaps desolateness a
people see a strength an
from intimate familiar
the land as a secure and
because tradition teach
the place where they are
—Emory Sekaquaptew

Hopi land will
starkness, and
around, the Hopi
l beauty that comes
ty with it. They see
friendly place
s them that this is
supposed to be . . .
u

Hopi Mesas

Hopi land is held in trust in a spiritual way for the Great Spirit, Massau'u. Sacred Hopi ruins are planted over the Four Corners area, including Black Mesa. This land is like the inner chamber of a church—our Jerusalem . . . This land was granted to the Hopi by a power greater than man can explain. Title is invested in the whole make-up of Hopi life. Everything is dependent on it. The land is sacred and if the land is abused, the sacredness of Hopi life will disappear and all other life as well . . .

To us, it is unthinkable to give up control over our sacred lands to no-Hopis. We have no ways to express the exchange of sacred lands for money. It is alien to our ways. The Hopis never gave authority to anyone to dispose of our lands and heritage and religion for any price. We received these lands from the Great Spirit and we must hold them for him, as a steward, a caretaker, until he returns.
—*Hopi Religious Leaders*

The driving force of the Hopi religion is the urgent need for water in any form, as rain for farming, for drinking water in the springs, or snow to replenish the land. Water is forever the primary motivation. To survive in this waterless land the Hopi devised a complex religion to secure supernatural assistance . . . One element of the multi-faceted religion is the Kachina Cult, with every Hopi [male] past the age of ten being an initiated member. The basic concept of the cult is that all things in the world have two forms, the visible object and a spiritual counterpart, a dualism that balances mass and energy. Kachinas are the spirit essence of everything in the real world. Their existence is inferred from the steam which rises from food and whose loss does not change the form of the food, to the mist rising from a spring on a cold morning or the cloud which forms above a mountain top.
—*J. Brent Ricks and Alexander E. Anthony Jr.*

Children were taught th[...]
to be defined in actions[...]
In talking to children, t[...]
place a hand on the gro[...]
"We sit in the lap of our[...]
and all other living thin[...]
pass, but the place wher[...]
forever." —Chief Luthe[...]

at true politeness was
rather than in words . . .
e old Lakota would
nd and explain:
Mother. From her we,
gs, come. We shall soon
we now rest will last
Standing Bear

Chaco Canyon

Chaco—heart of Anasazi civilization—was built on a spectacular scale. More than 75 carefully engineered structures of up to 600 rooms were connected by a network of roads in a complex regional system of trade and ceremonial life. Water-control berms and channels made possible extensive farming of the arid valley. Many astronomical alignments have been found at Chaco, both in the buildings and marked by petroglyphs among the tumbled boulders of the surrounding terrain. This was a civilization close to both earth and sky. The hallmark of Chacoan civilization was the great kiva: huge, elaborate, and central in the arrangement of the pueblo. Elements included a series of niches around the walls, which in some cases held loops of precious shell or turquoise. Encircling benches may have been for people, or, as in some kivas today, only for spirits. Pairs of floor vaults, oriented north-south, made booming drums when covered with planking—and may also have been used to sprout seeds for ceremonies. An antechamber in the north side held an entryway . . .
—*Susan Lamb and Chuck Place*

It is not alone for the beauty of its surfaced rocks, for the invention of the staircase, and the roofing of cedar slabs worked smooth as planed boards, with, as yet, no knives but stone, that the Chaco ruins are distinguished, but for the evidence of high social organization in its defense and its adaptation to civic and religious group life . . . There was an art of inlaying at Chaco, turquoise and pink stone and lignite on wood and bone, there were painted flutes of four notes, trumpets of murexshell by which the rain priests called the rain, and the beginnings of that subtle art invented once by the Chinese and nowhere else in the world, the art of cloisonné. —*Mary Austin*

Pueblo Bonito, probably the largest single prehistoric Indian building in the Southwest at the time it was constructed, represents the highest development of Anasazi architecture. Most of the construction was between the years A.D. 1030 and 1079 . . . The Navajos, who were not here until long after the last of the Anasazi departed, call Pueblo Bonito "the place where the cliff is propped up," and they relate a tale about their predecessors pouring baskets of turquoise and white shell behind the rock as an offering to the spirits to prevent its fall. When the huge slab finally came down in January 1941, no turquoise was found, but it was discovered that the Anasazi had placed prayer sticks behind the rock. These are peeled and carved willow wands, painted and decorated with feathers, which are still used by Pueblo people somewhat in the way altar candles are used.
—*National Park Service*

Opposite and overleaf:
Pueblo Bonito
Second overleaf: Badlands
near Chaco Canyon

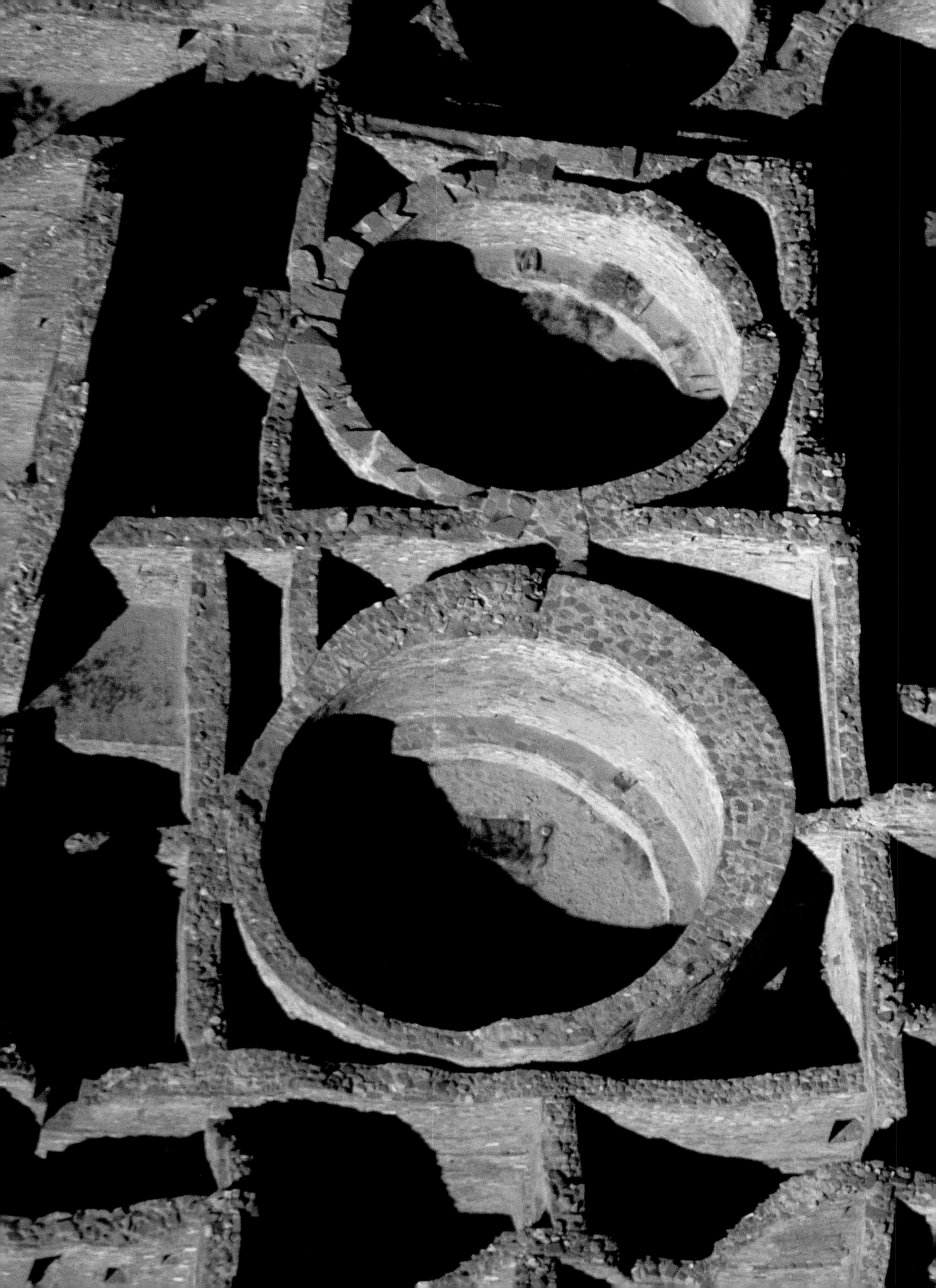

Whatever the cause, the
the effect. The desert air
air. Several times from
seen it lying below me l
cloud or veil. A similar
or pale yellow is to be se
Grand Canyon . . . The
and dust control the ap
the sky at dawn is as po
pearly grays just emerg
again it may be flushed
and pink . . . —John C.

e can be no doubt about

is practically colored

igh mountains I have

ke an enormous tinted

eiling of pink, lilac,

n in the gorges of the

prices of light, heat,

earances. Sometimes

lid as a snowdrop with

ng from the blue; and

with saffron, rose,

Van Dyke

Desert Light

Every part of this soil i
Every hillside, every va
grove has been hallowe
event in days long vani
now stand on responds
footsteps than to yours,
the blood of our ancesto
conscious of the sympa
—Chief Seattle

sacred to my people.
ley, every plain and
by some sad or happy
hed. The very dust you
nore willingly to their
because it is rich with
s and our bare feet are
hetic touch.

Canyon de Chelly

What I am trying to say is hard to tell and hard to understand . . . unless, unless . . . you have been yourself at the edge of the deep Canyon and have come back unharmed. Maybe it all depends on something within yourself—whether you are trying to see the Watersnake or the sacred Cornflower, whether you go out to meet death or to Seek Life. It is like this; as long as you stay within the realm of the great Cloudbeings, you may indeed walk at the very edge of the Deep Canyon and not be harmed. You will be protected by the rainbow and by the Great Ones. You will have no reason to worry and no reason to be sad. You may fight the witches, and if you can, meet them with a heart which does not tremble, the fight will make you stronger. It will help you to attain your goal in life; it will give you strength to help others, to be loved and liked, and to Seek Life.
—*Vera Laski*

I think that I understa[n...]
before what it is that [th...]
deserts] do to the soul, [w...]
more than merely aesth[...]
why its spaciousness as[...]
are more than merely p[...]
nervously—reassuring[...]
to approve and to encou[...]
which I have found scar[...]
men, and of which I ha[...]
quite so sure that even [...]
—Joseph Wood Krutch

d better than I did

e Southwestern

hy I find this country

tically satisfying, and

well as its austerity

ysically—and

. . . The desert seems

rage an attitude with

t sympathy among

e never before been

ature approved . . .

Sunset Crater
and Wupatki

Sunset Crater, with the grace and flow of a lasting sunset, was not always so serene, for 900 years ago it violently erupted and frightened the people away. But it was also kind, for it spread upon the earth an ash that enriched the soil. The people came back . . . Villages were established throughout the area. One of the longest inhabited is now called Wupatki, the Hopi word for "tall house." Its location was probably determined by the presence of a spring, one of the few in this region . . . Wupatki grew to be the largest in the area—during the 1100s it contained more than 100 rooms and, in places, was three stories high . . . They lived here for two centuries until the very winds that spread the "magic" ash stripped it from the soil. And then the people left . . . forever.
—*National Park Service*

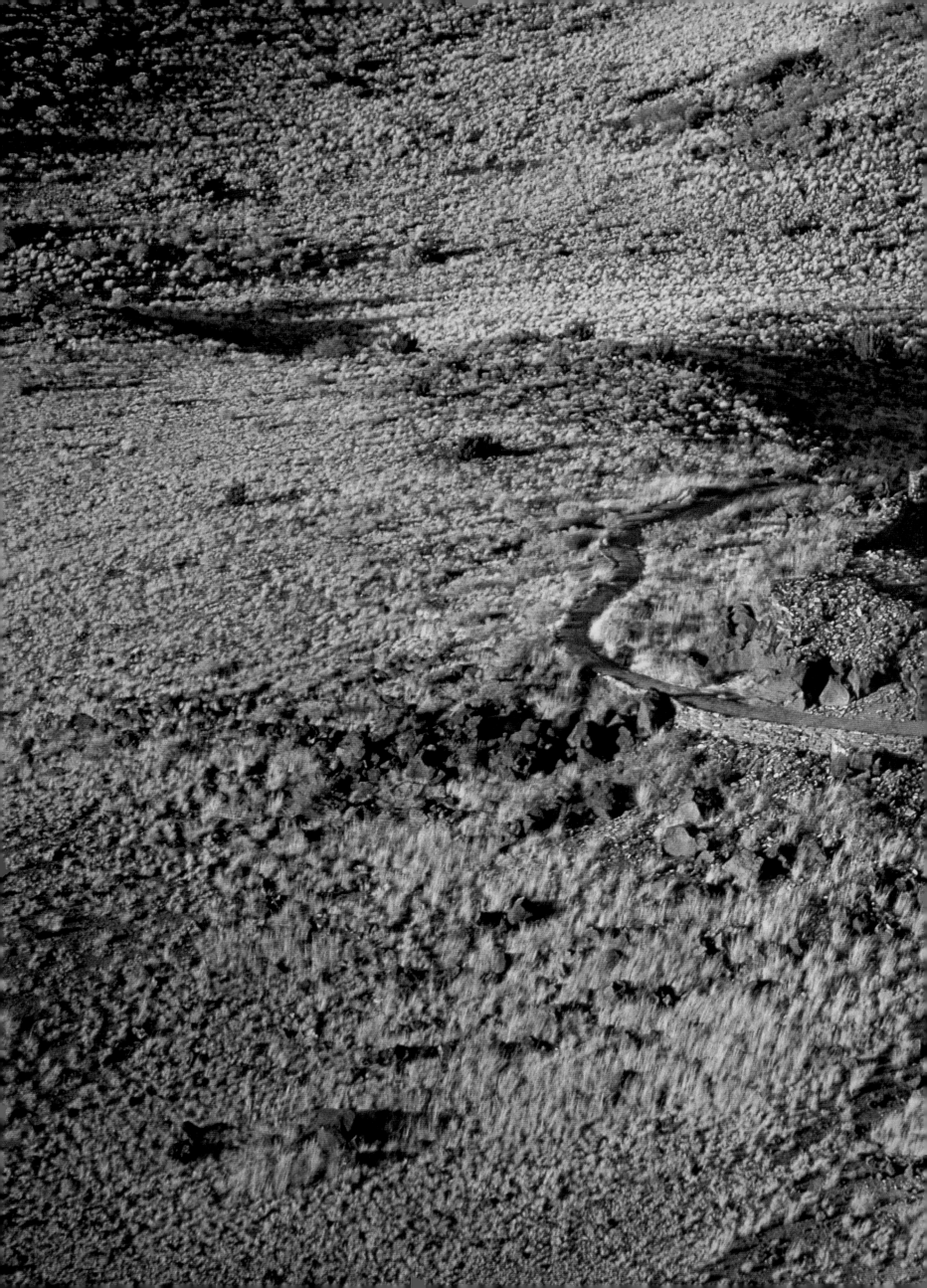

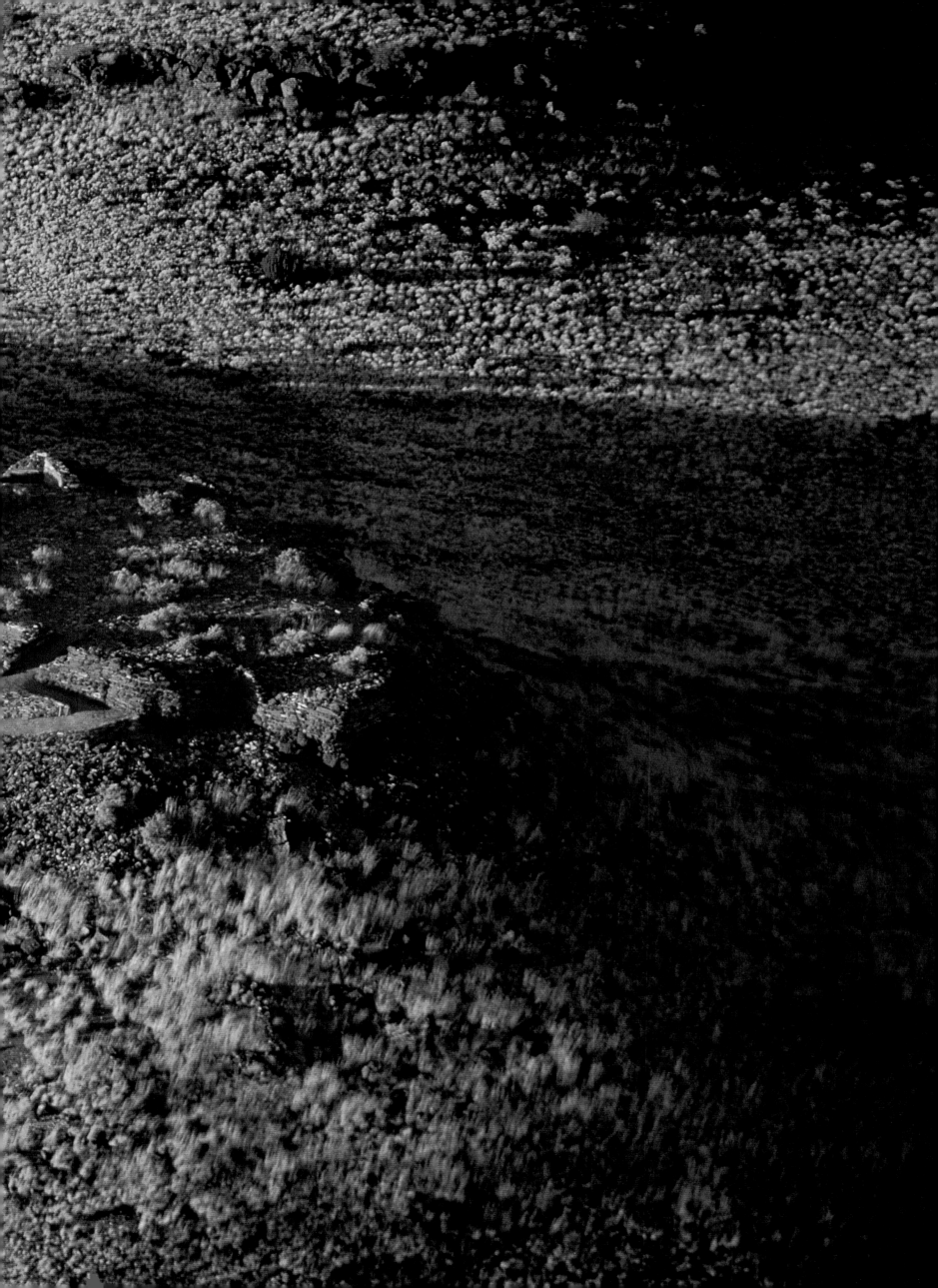

Here the mountains hav
At one moment you are
ice-cold waterfalls, and t
looking down again on s
Around the floor of the c
bright in the sunlight, w
of red sandstone . . . It wo
very remote but very fri
not quite in this world. –

married the desert . . .
mong the firs and the
e next moment you are
nd and cactus . . .
nyons, very sharp and
re great twisted shapes
all strangely beautiful,
ndly, like some place
-J. B. Priestly

Sedona

Traditional Navajo me
human beings everywh
dimension of time in th
cosmic level, however, t
sheds such mortal, hum
and manifests itself in t
Within the vastness of t
underlying cyclical nat
to spiritually attuned N
flow of events and proce
—David Suzuki and Pe

and women, like

re, experience a linear

ir daily lives . . . At a

e Navajo notion of time

an-centered illusions

ne purity of a circle.

e whole universe, the

ure of time is apparent

avajo in the dynamic

sses of nature.

er Knudtson

Acoma Pueblo

Francisco Vásquez de Coronado's army visited Acoma in the year 1540. The first white man to enter Sky City, he described Acoma as: "One of the strongest ever seen, because the city was built on a high rock. The ascent was so difficult that we repented climbing to the top." Sky City is considered an ideal site for defense against enemies. The oral heritage of Acoma tells of the origin and migration of Acoma people in search of HaK'u . . . It was prophesied from the beginning that there existed a place ready for the people to occupy. HaK'u means in a sense to prepare or plan. Archaeologists theorize that Acoma was occupied around A.D. 1150. It is considered the oldest continuously inhabited city in the United States.
—*Visitor's Guide*

In the house of long life,
In the house of happine[ss]
Beauty before me, with
Beauty behind me, with
Beauty below me, with
Beauty above me, with
Beauty above me, with
Beauty all around me,
In old age traveling, wi[th]
I am on the beautiful tr[ail]
—Washington Matthew[s]

there I wander.

s, there I wander.

t I wander.

it I wander.

t I wander.

I wander.

t I wander.

vith it I wander.

h it I wander.

uil, with it I wander.

s

Petrified Forest and
Painted Desert

A drive through the park is an invitation to "Visit the Triassic"—an opportunity to step back in time, to walk through Crystal or Rainbow forests, to view the eroded terrain at Blue Mesa, and to puzzle over the petroglyphs near the Puerco Ruin . . . Invariably it is the visitor's own sense of wonder and curiosity that grows from these encounters with the geological and prehistoric past preserved at Petrified Forest. —*George M. Lubick*

For the Navajos, everything the eye meets reflects the presence of deities or supernatural. That is as true of the San Francisco Peaks as it is of the recesses and ridges on the Painted Desert. It applies to the high mesas and tiny stones, to rivers and washes. The whole world testifies to the activity of spirits, whose role is to establish and maintain something called hozhó . . . The word means something like harmony, beauty, and balance all wrapped in one concept that dwells at the heart of the Navajo world view. —*Paul G. Zolbrod*

Opposite and overleaf:
Petrified Forest

Shall I take a knife and
bosom? Then when I di
her bosom to rest. You a
Shall I dig under her sk
when I die I cannot ent
again. You ask me to cu
and sell it, and be rich l
dare I cut off my mothe

tear my mother's
she will not take me to
k me to dig for stone!
n for her bones? Then
r her body to be born
grass and make hay
ke white men! But how
's hair? —Wovoka

Monument Valley

Spider Woman instructed the Navajo women how to weave on a loom which Spider Man told them how to make. The crosspoles were made of sky and earth cords, the warp sticks of sun rays, the heddles of rock crystal and sheet lightning. The batten was a sun halo, white shell made the comb. There were four spindles: one a stick of zigzag lightning with a whorl of cannel coal; one a stick of flash lightning with a whorl of turquoise; a third had a stick of sheet lightning with a whorl of abalone; a rain streamer formed the stick of the fourth, and its whorl was white shell.
—*Navajo Legend*

I put a lot of thinking into it. Even at night, I think about how I'm going to weave. Thinking about how I want to make it makes my head ache—thinking about how nice the weaving will be. It's the same as when a man is building a house and he gets very tired, or a man might be working very hard on the railroad. Weaving's like doing the same kind of hard work. —*Ason Yellowhair*

Opposite: Totem Pole
Pages 180–81: Spearhead Lake
Overleaf: Mittens

It is through the power
of eye and ear, of tongue
that a place first rises u
afterwards it is memor
that allows it to grow in
For as long as our recor
these two things dear, lo
Each infuses us with a
—Barry Lopez

f observation, the gifts
and nose and finger,
in our mind;
that carries the place,
depth and complexity.
ds go back, we have held
ndscape and memory.
ifferent kind of life.

My Camera Above the Southwest
Harvey Lloyd

The airplane has unveiled for us the true face of the earth. —*Antoine de Saint-Exupéry*

I wrote the following notes and observations during my aerial adventures with collaborator Shirlee Price and also as a summation of my own convictions about the power of photography to interpret the landscape. The technical information about flight and photography is linked to my personal feelings about the desert landscapes—they are the same.

The photographs in this section are some of my personal favorites from the book and hold special memories for me. As I took these photographs, I had the feeling that my journeys over the lands of the Southwest were somehow ordained—that I was somehow blessed and kept aloft by the hand of the great spirit.

The art of photography rests on a foundation of composition, the ability to see the frame entire, to perceive the patterns of asymmetric composition and tension, to hold those patterns. You must discover and rediscover these images while firing off a large number of shots to make sure that you are bracketing the film exposures and getting enough different ones to ensure that you will be safe and sure of success. I often shoot three, four, or five rolls on any important subject, partly because the imagery keeps changing, the point of view keeps changing, and partly because I employ a fail-safe method of redundancy to guarantee that there is something on the film correctly exposed under often difficult lighting conditions.

Mesa Verde
Bill Moore, a bear of a pilot from Cortez, Colorado, thunders his turbocharged Cessna 210 straight at Mesa Verde. We wheel high atop the eagle's domain, the ruined pueblos of the Anasazi, ancient ones, basketmakers and tillers of the desert during the dark ages of Europe, architects of this elegant symmetry of rock and stone under the beetle-browed cliffs.

Early morning sunlight slants across Sun Temple on top of the mesa. We fly at the legal 1,500 feet above the ruins. I use my 400mm f/5.6 lens to get in close to the ruins, wishing that it were faster. (A fast 400mm lens is very expensive, huge, and heavy. I constantly struggle to pack all my gear into two big camera bags that can be carried into jet airplane cabins.) My big KS-8 gyro-stabilizer, or "invisible tripod," steadies the 400mm lens. With the gyro I can make sharp images at $^1/_{250}$ of a second with a long telephoto lens that should normally be fired at $^1/_{1000}$ of a second. It steadies the camera and dampens vibration and sudden aircraft movement. In addition, the gyro makes it easy to frame and keep the composition of the image intact while the aircraft is wheeling through the sky. Without it, many low-light dawn, sunrise, and sunset aerial photographs in this book could not have been made from the unstable platform of a speeding aircraft.

At the moment of truth in your photography, when you are somersaulting on a balance beam of split-second decisions, you have no room for error. There is no opportunity, there is no time in those fleeting seconds to think because, especially at dawn and sunset, there are brief moments when the light is enchanting, magical. You must react spontaneously, like an Olympic athlete. That takes pure intuitive instinct, training, reflexes disciplined to the limit. Photography demands that a mature mind and a delicate, sensitive perception be yoked to such finely honed reflexes, a process of training as demanding as training for the Olympics. I believe that it takes twenty or thirty or forty years of constant practice to reach that level in photography!

Those trained instincts are all you can depend upon when you are on that critical razor's edge of making visual discoveries and capturing them on film. You bring to it all of your training, all of your knowledge, all of your education, all of the many years of attempting to do these things, all of the immediate and quick reflexive responses of your muscles and your eye. You unleash your ability to recognize instantaneously patterns that are meaningful, patterns that make the kind of images that you are often not aware of at the time. When you are working instinctively and intuitively, you don't know what you've seen and photographed much of the time until you come back and see the film. Then, when the passion and adrenaline have gone, when you have left that trancelike state, you can soberly discover what you have either achieved or not achieved. You learn how much you know and how much you still have to learn. Those are the moments of discoveries, of epiphanies, when you realize that you have seen things that neither you nor anyone else you know of has seen or has been able to see and capture in that manner. That is the challenge of all serious photography, but certainly from my standpoint it is one of the great challenges of aerial photography.

Sedona and Sunset Crater
The airport at Sedona perches on Table Top or, as it is called, Airport Mesa. Kevin, a young blond pilot, welcomes us. As we take off, the red rocks of Sedona shimmer below us in the afternoon sun. The majestic landscape is dotted with housing developments. I am saddened at this desecration of one of nature's wonders. Formations fit for a national park stand next to new houses. A church dominates a crag surrounded by sculpted rocks. I photograph this stunning canyon that, from the air, from this angle, shows little sign of human works.

We fly out of Sedona and over the Mogollon Rim toward the nearby San Francisco Peaks, Flagstaff, and Sunset Crater. When the earth belched fire, smoke, and lava, Sunset Crater's basalt cone rose a thousand feet into the air, a fiery red whale breaching the dust-darkened skies. Gently rounded now, the crater glows yellow and red at the top from deposits of gypsum, sulphur, and iron oxide. Spatter cones, squeeze-ups, and lava bubbles surround the cone. First active around 1064 A.D., Sunset Crater is the youngest cinder cone in the United States. Eruptions yet to come, patient and fiery, bubble beneath this hot spot in the earth's mantle.

Hidden from ground level but clearly in view from our aerial vantage point, Sunset Crater's companion, a black, polished, and rounded lava flow, circles down toward us, forming a huge S-curve. The late-day shadows etch scimitars of black into the crater and the lava flow cone. I seek the exact position in the air that will enable me to photograph this confluence of abstractions, this black rock surplice and green-yellow crater, with the delicacy that the natural geometry demands. After half a dozen circles, seventy-degree banks, and turns, we sail on past the craters, on target. I fire thirty-six exposures during the few seconds that the arcs, parabolas, and sinuous curves form an elegant composition. We head back to Sedona for the sunset.

The canyon of rock formations flaunts an artist's palette of reds, red umber, and garnet, sanguine, ruddy red colors in the sun's dying light. We circle the canyon twice before the sun winks out. The ancient red rocks brood over a rude sprinkling of lights, pinpricks of housing that disturb eternity's sacred song.

Perception depends on the training of the eye. It hinges on an acquired historical perspective on fine art and photography that you carry with you, the knowledge of all varieties and transitions and various art forms, the concept of Eastern art, the concept of Zen, the concept of the Japanese word hacho, *which means "breaking the harmony." (The Japanese use this technique when making* ikebana, *Japanese floral arrangements.) You may see this dissonance or asymmetry when you visit in the stone gardens of the Zen temples such as the famous Ryoan-ji Temple in Kyoto where the rocks are incredibly balanced yet on the verge of unbalance, almost violent yet strangely peaceful. All of those things are in your unconscious mind when you are over a Zen temple as vast and sublime as the Colorado Plateau and you are photographing instinctively and intuitively.*

Opposite: Baby Rocks, Arizona
Pages 200–201:
Meteor Crater, Arizona

This page: Delicate Arch,
Arches National Park, Utah
Opposite: Sunset Crater,
Arizona

Overleaf: Angel Arch,
Canyonlands National
Park, Utah

Acoma Pueblo, Chaco Canyon,
Canyon de Chelly

In her book *Death Comes to the Archbishop*, Willa Cather tells of a Catholic priest living in the church at Acoma long ago. The priest, entertaining some missionaries and slightly tipsy, throws a silver mug at an Indian boy in his service. The boy falls dead. The priest's guests hurriedly leave via the single trail down the cliff. Several hours later, men of Acoma come to the priest's rooms, silently seize and bind him, and hurl him down from the cliff's edge.

A rush of ice-cold air greets me as the pilot, Jim, opens the window. We whirl in tight circles at 1,500 feet above the pueblo. I sit wedged in behind Jim's pilot seat and against Shirlee's front seat. I aim my 80–200mm zoom lens at "sky city" and fire away. Perched on a mesa, surrounded by sculpted rock formations, Acoma Pueblo gleams in yellow early morning sunlight. Long shadows outline the large Catholic church and the pueblo buildings. Tall rocks formations tower against the mesa, like flying buttresses.

Shirlee and I had contacted T. J. ("Jim") Sheppard a few days earlier. I questioned his tactics; he was polite but firm. "I fly from the right seat. You photograph behind me. The 210 has no wing spar. With the landing gear up, you have a clear field of vision!" My concerns about photographing from the rear seat assuaged, he met us early in the morning at the Gallup, New Mexico, airport. Once Jim is warmed up to his task, he flies the Cessna around Acoma with precision, making tight vertical turns and side-slipping into position for the photographs.

After about half an hour at Acoma we head for the great Anasazi ruins at Chaco Canyon. A week earlier, we flew from Grant, New Mexico, with another pilot and found Chaco Canyon, but could not spot the ruins. Jim says laconically, "Well, I hope I can find them." He is joking. "I've flown over these lands for twenty years, hundreds of times. We *may* find the ruins." Of course, we arrive precisely over the ruins of the Anasazi pueblos.

My photography complete, Jim flies to Canyon de Chelly on the Navajo reservation, another sixty miles or so away. Its gorge suddenly appears, a gigantic crack in the bleak, flat desert. Below the canyon rim, the river winds and winds, surrounded by verdant green meadows and trees. Black shadows etch the canyon walls. The White House ruins are tucked under a huge, curving overhang of rock. Streaks of reddish brown and black desert varnish reach down toward the ruin. I wrestle with the gravity forces and with the torque of the gyro. My target slides into place at the bottom of the vast white rock overhang.

Jim carves an elegant symmetry in the still air. His delicate touch on the yoke that steers the aircraft enables him to feel for the winds like an eagle, responding to the slightest air currents. This short, elderly man possesses deft and sensitive responses honed by many long years at the controls. He knows where I must be at each moment. He sees what I see and he anticipates my needs. We whirl about on a feather-bed roller coaster, delicately urged into position, not bounced or battered. Jim tells us that he flies tight turns for hundreds of hours over forest fires, spotting blazes for fire fighters. "Just about the same as I'm doing now," he drawls over the intercom. Rarely have I encountered the almost invisible skill, the special talent and ease with the machine that makes an aircraft fly so that it resembles a bird in its careful movements, in the eloquence of its flight.

The art of photography is the absorption and immersion of your total being into what you are photographing. You and it are no longer apart; you have become one. In the Eugene Herrigel book Zen and the Art of Archery, *the student asked the master, "How do I let loose the arrow?" The master looked at him and said simply, "It shoots."*

It *is you when you are one with the* landscape. It *is you when you are one with your camera. You are in a trance and* it shoots.

Arches

Dale Ogden, friend and pilot, greets us at Moab's tiny airport. Shirlee loads gear into the Cessna 207, a brute of a single engine aircraft, capable of lifting 1,700 pounds of freight, luggage, and passengers. Dale's handshake is like a vise. He tells me that we fly the 207 because the 182 needs parts and the 172 is not yet fully put back together. They tried to get it ready for me, but a few parts still need installing. "Hey," I say to Dale, "don't rush them."

We take off to circle Arches National Park. Dale is a photographer's pilot. He intuitively knows how to position the big 207 precisely where I need it. A good pilot makes aerial photography easy. An inexperienced pilot hurls you all over the sky, usually to the wrong place. It's a matter of orientation, of spatial smarts. Some pilots have it; many don't.

Shirlee sits in the rear seat, surrounded by a camera store full of equipment, lenses, camera bodies, film, polarizers, and filters. She holds the window open with her gloved hand. The temperature outside is about 20 degrees Fahrenheit, and the wind chill about twenty below.

We fly at about 170 miles per hour straight for the park, fifteen minutes away. If my timing is right, we will make it in time for a flame of sunset light on the red rocks. We are almost too late. Our Cessna claws the thin air to climb to 12,000 feet over the foothills of the La Sal mountains. To the east, away from the setting sun, a pale band of light appears over the peaks. Winter light! Mauve, pink, red, and purple, like a Peruvian sash, like a light show, like a painting by Monet.

How well you are able to execute your creation is a matter of time and hard work and constant seeking after the Holy Grail of individuality, of creativity, of originality, of all the things that are possible but are very, very difficult and that make for the finest kind of work. That passion comes from accepting a certain way of life as a calling, as an investiture, from devoting all of your energy to it. If your art or your creativity is photography then the result itself—the artwork, the print, the photograph—must express your passion.

Hopi Mesas

Until we flew over them, I knew the Hopi Mesas only from a few black-and-white ground-level photographs. From the ground, against a dawn sky, the pueblo's buildings seemed typical of pueblos anywhere, the landscape nondescript. But in Bill Yoder's Cessna 182RG (retractable gear) with the bright red seats and cushions we soar over a moonscape scribed with strange markings, erosion's mythology or archaeology. Twenty minutes before sunset, we view the mesas. Bill is not entirely sure which is which—First Mesa, Second Mesa, Third Mesa. I am startled by what I see.

The rocky ramparts below the Hopi Mesas crash like sandy waves against the plateau tops. Deeply eroded, carved, gouged, and sundered, the seascape of rock glows yellow. Beyond the canyons, above the tempest of stone, the pueblos perch delicately, life rafts of stone. Below lies the sacred, the mysterious, the holy world of the Hopis. Within those walls occur dances and ceremonies rarely seen by outsiders.

We do not fly low. That would violate the traditional Hopi laws. I use telephoto lenses, 80–200mm f/2.8 and 300mm f/2.8, to frame the rockbound, shipwrecked, sacred setting of the Hopi pueblos. The light softens and diminishes. The pueblos flare red. I steady the camera and fire away.

When someone says that the Colorado Plateau has been photographed many, many times, and indeed it has, as has all of the Southwest and Northwest and Great West, and that it has become something of a cliché, I respond that nature is never a cliché because of constant change; the light is never the same, the color is never the same. Just as

Heraclitus said, "the same river never runs twice," the same light never occurs twice, the same point of view never occurs twice, the same intensity of emotion and ability to create an abstract composition from the chaotic variety of nature never happens twice in the same way.

Canyonlands and Lake Powell

I awake from slightly dizzy reverie—oxygen deprivation at ten thousand feet—fire the camera, and wave the pilot, Michael, on to Canyonlands. Slithery, muddy brown in the dying light, the confluence of the Green and Colorado Rivers slides by below, interwoven like a measureless Möbius strip, a ribbon twined in the petrified red hair of the Colorado Plateau. To the right I see Shirlee's favorite garden, the green meadows of the Needles surrounded by rocky spires and obelisks, and beyond, the trackless labyrinth of the Maze area.

We fly on, determined to return to Page by sunset. Michael asks me to fly the Cessna 210. I, no pilot, gently hold the yoke, *gently*, and feel the surge of the wind against the airfoils of the wings. I carefully move the yoke to raise and lower the nose, tilt wings slightly, as I might touch a slumbering giant, in love with the raw power and the infinite grace of flight. Soon, Lake Powell glistens among black rock monoliths and crags. A red sky bands the horizon. I let go of the murmuring yoke and lean out the window to photograph the last light of evening on the waters and the sky glow that reaches across the heavens, somnambulist of early evening.

You need to be aware that nature gives gifts. I think you must be grateful in front of an extraordinary morning like the one we had at the Grand Canyon the morning after a snowfall when the storm was clearing. There was an extraordinary epiphany at Hopi Point at sunset as the rain shower blew through the canyon in a bubble of golden light. The feeling when you encounter and see such things makes you feel blessed. We are privileged when we are up in the air at

dawn or sunset, when we fly through thunderstorms over Lake Powell, or the red dawn over Arches where the light is so beautiful, or the sunsets over Canyonlands. When you see something such as Shiprock revealed from the air, you are given bounty.

When you encounter those things that are gifts, you should feel the same sense of reverence you feel at a solemn mass at a cathedral, or at a concert of Mozart or Bach. You cannot impatiently approach nature with your eye on your watch; you have to be prepared to donate the time, the funds if necessary, to stay out there and wait. Then, when nature decides to give a gift, you are available, you are ready.

Monument Valley

Thirty minutes before sunset, Kyle, acrobatic pilot of our Cessna 182RG, spins the light aircraft into a dizzying descent around the Totem Pole and Yei Bi Chei rocks. I lean out of the window. Shadows march across the red desert floor like spirits of ghost dancers awakening from the afterlife. Our winged metal vessel dances in the shimmering yellow sunlight like a mayfly, ephemeral, for a few minutes of glorious flight, until the sun descends into the underworld. Kyle banks, twists, and turns, whirling the Cessna toward the stone "hands of the great spirit," the red rock mittens of Monument Valley. The earth tumbles beneath us. We veer and turn, a whirling dervish suspended in thin air, shadowed by the sun's grim burning.

Spires, castles, battlements, towers, and rock cliffs rear out of the red desert sand to embrace the dusk. In the distance are tiny red mounds, hogans that face east to greet each newborn day. We fleet across the picket line of monuments—King on his Throne, Stagecoach, Bear and the Rabbit, Big Indian. Their dying shadows sink into the parched land. The ancient ones doze again.

Opposite:
Canyonlands National Park, Utah
Pages 214–15:
North and South Windows, Arches National Park, Utah
Overleaf:
Pueblo Bonito, Chaco Canyon, New Mexico

Epilogue

Thinking back, I know that these desert landscapes are the closest thing to home that Shirlee and I encountered during our several million miles pilgrimage around the earth. Certain places call you home. You discover, inside of yourself, an acute sense of déjà vu, as though you had lived there before, a thousand or a hundred thousand years ago. To live truly is to seek, to find, and to open your heart. To live fully is to stay in tune with the earth, to feel respect for all living things, to perceive yourself as a part of the wheel of eternity, of the flowering of the universe. To live wisely is to partake of the sacred intelligence that permeates all things on earth. That gives meaning to our short span and echoes in resonance to the song of the earth.

I now know that there is only one blessed and complete bliss to be found in life. That is the joyous rite of homecoming.

Opposite:
Shiprock, New Mexico
Overleaf:
Monument Valley, Arizona

Excerpt Credits

Every effort has been made to secure the reprint rights to the excerpts reproduced in this book. Since some of the passages were not traceable, the publisher would be grateful to receive information from any copyright holder not credited herein. Omissions will be corrected in subsequent editions.

18 "The world before me . . .": Ron McCoy, *Plateau Magazine* (Museum of Northern Arizona).

18 "Hozhó . . . the word means . . .": Paul G. Zolbrod, *Plateau Magazine* (Museum of Northern Arizona).

19 "It is like this . . .": Tewa man from San Juan Pueblo to Vera Laski in Peggy V. Beck, Anna Lee Walters, and Nia Francisco, *The Sacred Ways of Knowledge, Sources of Life* (Navajo Community College Press, 1977).

19 "A cross section . . .": Ron Redfern, *The Making of a Continent.*

19 "Sun is our father . . .": Cecilia Etcitty in Terry Tempest Williams, *Pieces of White Shell.* Copyright © 1983, 1984 Terry Tempest Williams. Reprinted with the permission of Scribner, an imprint of Simon & Schuster, Inc.

22 "You look at that mountain . . .": Navajo man in Harvey Lloyd and Steven Trimble, *Our Voices, Our Land* (Flagstaff: Northland Press, 1986).

22 "We are the Stars which sing . . .": Algonquian, "Song of the Stars" in Gibbon, 1972.

26 "The life of these Indians . . .": de Angulo in Peggy V. Beck, Anna Lee Walters, and Nia Francisco, *The Sacred Ways of Knowledge, Sources of Life* (Navajo Community College Press, 1977).

26–27, 30–31 "This is coyote's country . . .": Terry Tempest Williams, *Pieces of White Shell.* Copyright © 1983, 1984 Terry Tempest Williams. Reprinted with the permission of Scribner, an imprint of Simon & Schuster, Inc.

36 "The Grand Canyon of the Colorado . . .": Clarence E. Dutton in Peter Wild, *The Desert Reader* (Salt Lake City: University of Utah Press, 1991).

40 "I focus quietly each day . . .": Excerpt from "Gone Back into the Earth" © 1981 by Barry Holstun Lopez, used with the permission of Sterling Lord Literistic. The full text appears in *Crossing Open Ground* by Barry Lopez.

44 "Imagine for a moment . . .": Arthur Versluis, *Sacred Earth: The Spiritual Landscape of Native America* (Rochester, N.Y.: Inner Traditions, 1992).

58–59 "Sometimes I dream this incipient lake . . .": Ann Weiler Walka, *Plateau Magazine* (Museum of Northern Arizona).

62 "Is it not of great significance . . .": Theodore Schwenk, *Sensitive Chaos: The Creation of Flowering Forms in Water and Air*, 1965.

72 "The verbal tradition . . .": N. Scott Momaday, "The Way to Rainy Mountain," *Plateau Magazine* (Museum of Northern Arizona).

90–91 "Listen to the air . . .": John Lame Deer in Paul B. Steinmetz, *Meditations with Native Americans—Lakota Spirituality* (Santa Fe: Bear & Company, 1984).

94 "Life dances in the womb . . .": Ramson Lomatewama, *Drifting Through Ancestor Dreams* (Flagstaff: Entrada Books, Northland Publishing).

100–101 "Oh, Male God! . . .": Washington Matthews, "The Night Chant," *Plateau Magazine* (Museum of Northern Arizona).

103 "A voice said: 'Grandson' . . .": Gerald Hausman, *Meditations with the Navajo* (Santa Fe: Bear & Company, 1987).

108 "More than 1,800 stone arches . . .": David W. Johnson, *Arches: The Story Behind the Scenery* (KC Publications, 1985).

114 "The caprices of light . . .": John C. Van Dyke, *From The Desert* (New York: Charles Scribner's Sons, 1901).

116 "In the Desert . . . the very fauna and flora . . .": Joseph Wood Krutch, *The Desert Year* (New York: Viking Press, 1970).

120–21 "Where a stranger to the Hopi land . . .": Emory Sekaquaptewa, "Stories from the Land," *Plateau Magazine* (Museum of Northern Arizona).

124 "Hopi land is held in trust . . .": Hopi religious leaders in Peter Knudtson and David Suzuki, *Wisdom of the Elders* (New York: Bantam Books, 1992).

124 "The driving force of the Hopi religion . . .": J. Brent Ricks and Alexander E. Anthony Jr., *Kachinas: Spirit Beings of the Hopis* (Avanyu Publishing, 1993).

126–27 "Children were taught that true politeness . . .": Chief Luther Standing Bear in Louise Mengelkoch and Kent Nerburn, *Native American Wisdom* (San Rafael: New World Library, 1991).

129 "Chaco—heart of Anasazi civilization . . .": Susan Lamb and Chuck Place, *Ancient Walls: Indian Ruins of the Southwest* (Golden, Colo.: Fulcrum Publishing, 1992).

129 "It is not alone for the beauty . . .": Mary Austin, *The Land of Journeys' Ending* (Tucson: University of Arizona Press, 1983).

130 "Pueblo Bonito, probably the largest . . .": National Park Service.

136–37 "Whatever the cause . . .": John C. Van Dyke, *From The Desert* (New York: Charles Scribner's Sons, 1901).

144–45 "Every part of this soil is sacred . . .": Chief Seattle, Suqwamish and Duwamish, in Louise Mengelkoch and Kent Nerburn, *Native American Wisdom* (San Rafael: New World Library, 1991).

147 "What I am trying to say . . .": Vera Laski, *Seeking Life*, 1959.

150–51 "I think that I understand better . . .": Joseph Wood Krutch, *The Desert Year* (New York: Viking Press, 1970).

153 "Sunset Crater, with the grace and flow . . .": National Park Service.

156–57 "Here the mountains have married the desert . . .": J. B. Priestly, *Midnight on the Desert*, 1937.

162–63 "Traditional Navajo men and women . . .": David Suzuki and Peter Knudtson, *Wisdom of the Elders* (New York: Bantam Books, 1992).

166 "Francisco Vásquez de Coronado's army . . .": Acoma Pueblo visitor's guide.

170–71 "In the house of long life . . .": Washington Matthews, "Navaho Myths, Prayers and Songs," 1907.

173 "A drive through the park . . .": George M. Lubick, *Plateau Magazine* (Museum of Northern Arizona).

173 "For the Navajos, everything the eye meets . . .": Paul G. Zolbrod, *Plateau Magazine* (Museum of Northern Arizona).

178–79 "Shall I take a knife . . .": Wovoka, Paiute, in Louise Mengelkoch and Kent Nerburn, *Native American Wisdom* (San Rafael: New World Library, 1991).

190 "Spider Woman instructed . . .": Navajo legend in *Plateau Magazine* (Museum of Northern Arizona).

190 "I put a lot of thinking into it . . .": Ason Yellowhair in *Plateau Magazine* (Museum of Northern Arizona).

196–97 "It is through the power of observation . . .": Excerpt from "The American Geographies" © 1989 by Barry Holstun Lopez, used with the permission of Sterling Lord Literistic.